SPACE SHUTTLE

by Darlene R. Stille

Content Adviser: James Gerard, Aerospace Education Specialist,
Aerospace Education Services Program,
Merritt Island, Florida

Reading Adviser: Dr. Linda D. Labbo,
Department of Reading Education, College of Education,
The University of Georgia

Compass Point Books

Minneapolis, Minnesota

Compass Point Books
3109 West 50th Street, #115
Minneapolis, MN 55410

Visit Compass Point Books on the Internet at *www.compasspointbooks.com* or e-mail your request to *custserv@compasspointbooks.com*

Photographs ©: NASA, cover, 1, 4, 8, 10, 12, 14, 16, 18, 22, 24, 26; DigitalVision, 6, 20.

Editor: Christianne C. Jones
Photo Researcher: Svetlana Zhurkina
Designers: Melissa Kes/Jaime Martens

Library of Congress Cataloging-in-Publication Data
Stille, Darlene R.
  Space shuttle / by Darlene R. Stille.
        p. cm. — (Transportation)
Includes index.
Summary: A simple introduction to the space shuttle, describing its equipment, parts, uses, and journey into space.
  ISBN 0-7565-0609-3 (hardcover)
  1. Space shuttles—Juvenile literature. [1. Space shuttles.] I. Title. II. Series.
  TL795.515.S75 2004
  629.44'1—dc22   2003012305

Table of Contents

NOTE: In this book, words that are defined in the glossary
are in **bold** the first time they appear in the text.

launch
platform

crawler

4

The Countdown

Many people are getting the shuttle ready to go into space. This process is called the countdown.

A space shuttle will soon blast off from the Kennedy Space Center in Florida. The countdown begins.

The space shuttle starts in the **hangar.** A **crawler** moves the space shuttle and the launch platform to the launch pad. The shuttle takes off from the launch pad.

rockets

engines

launch pad

Liftoff!

The space shuttle looks like an airplane standing on end. Big rockets are strapped to the shuttle. The shuttle has three main engines.

"Five, four, three, two, one, liftoff!" A loud thunder sound fills the air. Fire shoots out from the big rockets, and the ground shakes.

Slowly, the shuttle starts moving. It starts to go faster and higher. The rockets leave a trail that looks like white smoke. Finally, the shuttle disappears into the sky.

Astronaut Training

All astronauts train for many years before going into space. Some of the training takes place in large water tanks. The water helps the astronauts adjust to being weightless in space.

Some astronauts are mission specialists. Mission specialists include doctors, engineers, and scientists. They learn to do special jobs on the space shuttle.

Flying the Shuttle

The **commander** and the pilot fly the shuttle. They watch the dials and computer screens for information. The dials and computers help them fly the shuttle.

A shuttle pilot must train for many years. Most shuttle pilots flew jet planes in the Army, Navy, or Air Force before joining the space program. Pilots can become commanders after their first shuttle flight.

Going into Orbit

The rockets strapped on the shuttle drop off. The shuttle is on its way into space!

When the shuttle moves fast, a force pushes the astronauts back in their seats. When the shuttle slows down, the pushing force is gone. Now the shuttle is in **orbit**.

The astronauts take off their seat belts. They are weightless and start to float around! There is no **gravity** to hold them down.

Living in Orbit

Living without gravity is tough.
Everything on the shuttle floats.
Astronauts eat, sleep, and work
while floating.

Astronauts use straws to drink.
They add water to dry food when
it is time to eat. The wet food sticks
in the plastic package.

Astronauts are strapped into beds
at night to sleep. They can also be
strapped down to work.

Doing Tests in Space

Scientists want to know how plants grow in orbit. Doctors want to know how your heart beats in orbit.

Astronauts study plants and animals on shuttle missions. They do tests on each other. They want to know if people, plants, or animals can live in space.

Mission specialists do tests to find out more about space. They want to answer the questions scientists and doctors have.

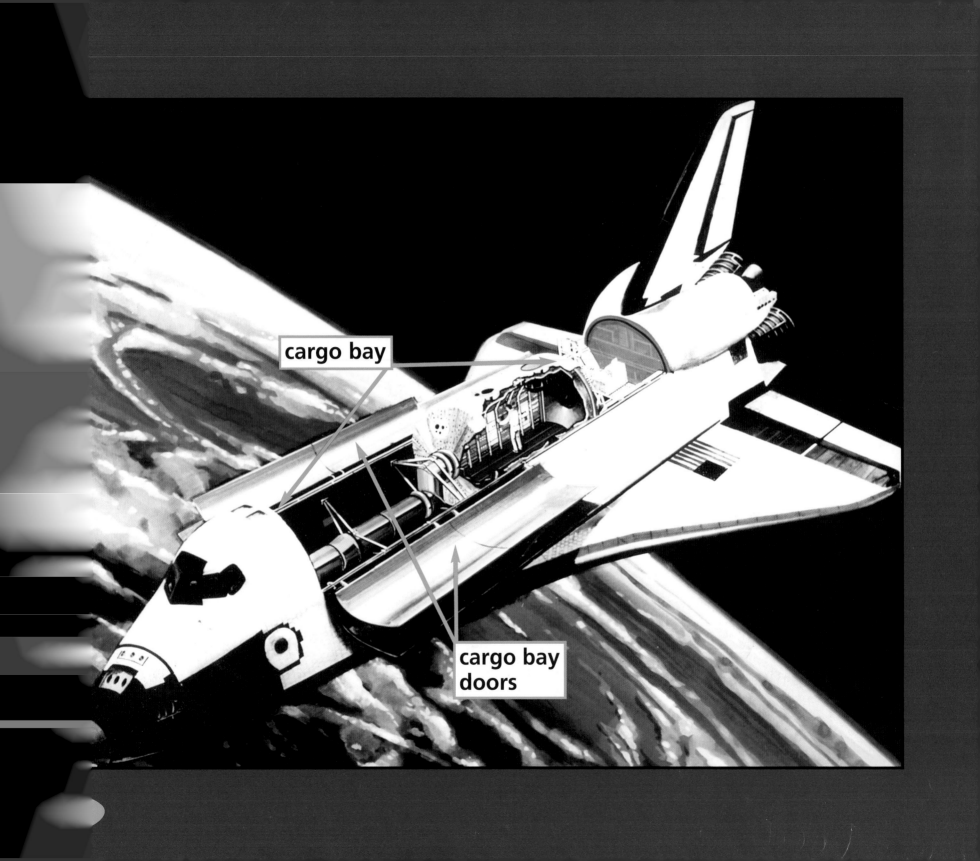

What's in the Cargo Bay?

The space shuttle carries **satellites** and other things in its cargo bay. The cargo bay is also called the payload bay. The cargo bay is large enough to hold an entire school bus!

Big doors cover the cargo bay. Astronauts open the doors when they are in orbit.

On this mission, the shuttle is carrying new parts for the International **Space Station.**

robot arm

Using a Robot Arm

The robot arm can do many things. Astronauts inside the shuttle control the arm. It can put a satellite into orbit. It can also catch a satellite and put it back into the cargo bay.

An astronaut can be attached to the robot arm. The astronaut moves around in space with help from the robot arm.

Sometimes the robot arm has a camera attached to the end of it. This makes it easy to look outside the shuttle.

helmet

oxygen
tank

straps

A Special Suit

Astronauts need to wear space suits when they go outside of the space shuttle. The suits keep them from getting too hot or too cold.

Astronauts also wear big helmets. Because there is no air in space, the helmets have oxygen tanks attached to them. The oxygen tanks pump air into the helmets so the astronauts can breathe.

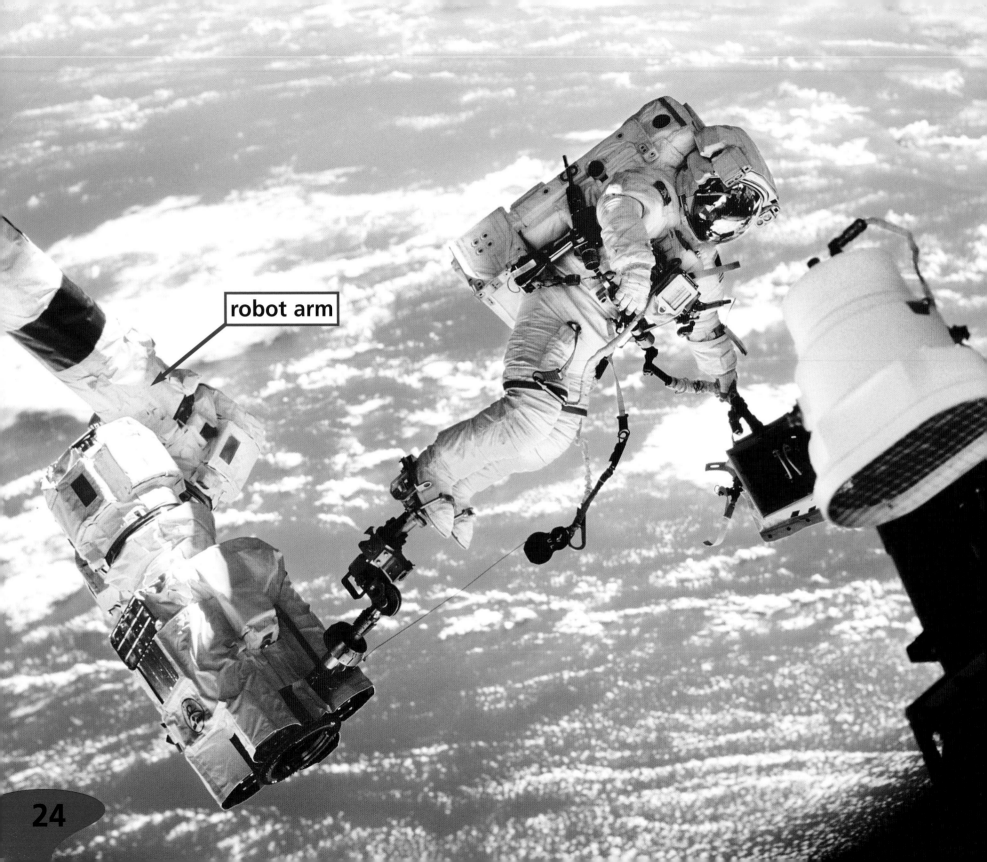

robot arm

Fixing a Space Station

An astronaut heads toward the International Space Station on the robot arm. The astronaut has new parts for the space station.

The astronaut replaces the old parts and fixes the space station. Mission accomplished. Now it is time to go back to Earth.

Returning to Earth

The astronauts fasten their seat belts. The pilot fires up the engines. The shuttle starts its trip back to Earth.

The shuttle gets very hot as it speeds toward Earth. The shuttle has a special covering to keep it from burning up.

The pilot heads for the long runway at Kennedy Space Center in Florida. Touchdown! A parachute opens behind the shuttle to slow it down. The mission is complete.

Glossary

commander—the main person in charge

crawler—a large vehicle that moves on steel belts and carries other large vehicles

gravity—the force that pulls all objects to the center of Earth

hangar—a building used for housing or repairing aircraft

orbit—to travel around an object in space

satellites—objects that orbit a planet

space station—a large satellite made for people to live in for long periods of time

Did You Know?

* After eight minutes, a space shuttle is moving at a speed of more than 17,000 miles (27,359 kilometers) per hour.

* If the main engines on a space shuttle used water instead of fuel, they would drain an average-size swimming pool every 25 seconds!

* A space shuttle takes off like a rocket, moves around Earth like a spaceship, and lands like an airplane.

* It takes 11 people to drive the crawler that moves the space shuttle.

* More than 14,000 people are involved in preparing a space shuttle for launch.

* NASA has been working on a smaller, simpler spacecraft. It would only have four seats. NASA has been working to develop a safer spacecraft to prevent shuttle disasters. On February 1, 2003, the Columbia shuttle broke apart during re-entry over Texas. Seven astronauts were killed.

Want to Know More?

At the Library

Bredeson, Carmen. *Living on a Space Shuttle.* New York: Children's Press, 2003.

Feldman, Heather. *Columbia: The First Space Shuttle.* New York: Powerkids Press, 2003.

Lassieur, Allison. *The Space Shuttle.* New York: Children's Press, 2000.

Wilson-Max, Ken. *Big Silver Space Shuttle.* New York: Scholastic, 1998.

On the Web

For more information on space shuttles, use FactHound to track down Web sites related to this book.

1. Go to *www.compasspointbooks. com/facthound*
2. Type in this book ID: 0756506093
3. Click on the *Fetch It* button.

Your trusty FactHound will fetch the best Web sites for you!

Through the Mail

American Institute of Aeronautics
and Astronautics (AIAA)
1801 Alexander Bell Drive
Suite 500
Reston, VA 20191
To learn about careers in the
space program

On the Road

Kennedy Space Center
Visitor Complex
Kennedy Space Center, FL 32899
Tour exhibits and learn about the
history of the space program

Index

About the Author

Darlene R. Stille is a science editor and writer. She has lived in Chicago, Illinois, all her life. When she was in high school, she fell in love with science. While attending the University of Illinois, she discovered that she also enjoyed writing. Today she feels fortunate to have a career that allows her to pursue both her interests. Darlene R. Stille has written more than 60 books for young people.